D1129769

Destination St Kilda

From Oban to Skye and The Outer Hebrides

Edited by Mark Butterworth

THE ISLANDS BOOK TRUST
Urras Leabhraichean Nan Eilean

Published in 2010 by The Islands Book Trust

www.theislandsbooktrust.com

Copyright remains with the named authors. Other than brief extracts for the purpose of review, no part of this publication may be reproduced in any form without the written consent of the publisher and copyright owner.

© The Islands Book Trust 2010

ISBN: 978-1-907443-03-9

British Library Cataloguing in Publication Data: A CIP record for this book can be obtained from the British Library.

All rights reserved. No part of this publication may be reproduced, stored in a retrieval system, or transmitted in any other form or by any means, electronic, mechanical, photocopying, recording or otherwise without the prior written permission of the publishers. This book may not be lent, hired out, resold or otherwise disposed of by way of trade in any form of binding or cover other than that in which it is published, without the prior consent of the publishers.

The Islands book Trust would like to thank Mark Butterworth and Michael Robson for their help with the production of this volume.

Cover design by Jim Hutcheson

Printed and bound by J F Print Ltd

All photographs © Mark Butterworth

Text © Mark Butterworth

The Islands Book Trust
Ravenspoint Centre
Kershader
South Lochs
Isle of Lewis
HS2 9QA
Tel: 01851 820946

THE ISLANDS BOOK TRUST
URRAS LEABHRAICHEAN NAN EILEAN

FOREWORD – THE HISTORICAL SETTING
By John Randall, Chairman, The Islands Book Trust

The Book Trust is very pleased to publish this volume. It contains, for the first time, the original text of two lectures, 'From Oban to Skye' and 'The Outer Hebrides' and the full set of accompanying hand-coloured lantern slides, produced by the George Washington Wilson Company of Aberdeen in the 1880s. The photographs were taken by George Washington Wilson and his colleague Norman Macleod when they travelled through the Hebrides to St Kilda in 1886.

As Mark Butterworth explains in his contributions, these lectures and slides took advantage of the latest technology of the time, and reflected a keen and growing demand in Victorian Britain for learning about different ways of life in various parts of the world, certainly not confined to Scotland. This interest was fuelled by rising incomes in the higher echelons of society and easier transport links and services, not least to the Hebrides.

As well as introducing some of the earliest photographs taken in the islands, which are of absorbing interest for their recording of contemporary life, the lecture notes are also of immense value because of the light they shed on how the Hebrides and their inhabitants were viewed amongst commentators from the outside world at this critical juncture in history.

The slides give us a vivid picture of social and economic life, housing conditions, agriculture and fishing in the islands in the 1880s. The black-house, the cas chrom, the creel and the bustle of the herring industry are all captured. So are everyday practices such as washing clothes outdoors, spinning and corn grinding by hand. While many of the photographs are obviously posed, they nonetheless offer a unique glimpse of a long-vanished era.

There are a few anomalies or questions which arise in relation to the slides. For example, Slide 45 appears to have been taken in Castlebay rather than Lochboisdale. Where is the Borve apparently featured in Slide 40? In all such cases, as in the text of the lectures, no changes have been made to the original versions.

Turning now to the commentary on and presentation of the pictures of the islands, the following key themes stand out:

— The images emphasise a sense of wonder at the natural beauty of the island landscape and seascape. The lecture notes make frequent reference to the barren and rocky nature of much of the Hebrides, and their isolation from more populous areas. We can see here the influence of the Romantic movement, which from the 18th century onwards came to regard wild scenery as a source of inspiration rather than horror.

— There is a clear tendency to pick out the spectacular and romantic, both in terms of natural features (eg Kilt Rock, Loch Coruisk), and associations with historical figures such as Bonnie Prince Charlie and Flora MacDonald. Victorian Britain had by the 1880s bought in wholesale to the mythology of the Highlands promoted by Sir Walter Scott.

— But at the same time much attention is given to the way of life of the ordinary islanders. While the tone is frequently patronising, if not occasionally insulting, the general approach is sympathetic towards the plight of the people. There is emphasis on their poverty, hard life, primitive living and working conditions, and apparent uncleanliness, but this is attributed at least partially to the injustices of landlords. This reflects the publicity given to Clearances and the Land Struggle through recent events such as the Battle of the Braes in Skye in 1882 and the setting up of the Napier Commission to enquire into the conditions of crofters in 1883.

— Nonetheless, there remains an assumption that the islanders are fundamentally different from the Lowland Scot, based on racial stereotypes clearly stated at the outset of the first lecture where the islanders are contrasted with the 'loyal, energetic, intelligent and practical (Lowland) Scotsman'. Such theories were prevalent at the time in Britain and Germany, developed by academics such as George Henderson. The confused incomprehension by visitors of the Gaelic language helped to reinforce this sense of difference.

— The attitude towards St Kilda, the ultimate destination, is an interesting combination of realistic observation and acceptance of conventional mythology. On the one hand, the lecture notes emphasise correctly that the language and habits of the natives of St Kilda were in many ways similar to those of their neighbours in the Outer Hebrides. On the other, they promote ideas only recently given currency by the journalist John Sands in the 1870s, such as the St Kilda Parliament and the Queen of St Kilda.

So, as we look at the slides and read the notes, we can get an impression of how visitors to the Hebrides regarded the islanders and their world at this particular point in history. The islands were becoming more accessible to an increasingly prosperous society. The dominant attitude was one of curiosity that such apparently primitive conditions could still be found in one part of Great Britain.

The inhabitants of the Hebrides were generally a subject for pity. It was becoming widely accepted that poor living conditions had been brought about through economic injustices, which needed to be corrected. But alongside this sympathy, which was at least less threatening than the overt hostility shown in earlier centuries, there was no feeling that the culture of the islanders was valuable or that the outsider could learn anything useful from their experience. The snatches of Gaelic phrases heard at the harbours seem to be regarded as symptomatic of a primitive society rather than as a window into the oral culture collected and celebrated by Alexander Carmichael in his 'Carmina Gadelica', first published in 1900.

I should like to thank all those who have helped towards this publication, particularly Mark Butterworth who owns the lecture notes and lantern slides, and has contributed the introduction about the George Washington Wilson company and the section about the origin and development of the magic lantern. Michael Robson provided helpful comments on some of the slides, and has compared the various versions of the lecture notes available in an effort to get the text reproduced here as close as possible to the originals.

Introduction

In June 1977 an auction house near Leeds, Yorkshire, offered a collection of "some" projection slides for sale. Numbering in excess of 35,000 glass photographic slides they were the old stock from the Bradford Company of Riley Brothers Limited. Famous at the end of the 19th century, Riley Brothers operated a significant business, claiming to be "The Largest Magic Lantern Outfitters in the World". The collection on offer was the remnants of their slide rental business and numbered over 700 wooden boxes, each containing about 50 3¼ inch square glass lantern or optical projection slides. The whole collection was purchased by a pair of slide enthusiasts and over the years dispersed among a larger number of collectors. Among the boxes was "Riley's Safety Despatch Box No: 133632" containing the set "From Oban to Skye and The Outer Hebrides" consisting of 62 (from a set of 67) lantern slides, hand coloured, complete with their original printed lecture notes. In 2004 Mark Butterworth acquired this set of slides from one of the original enthusiasts who bought the entire collection.

The images and text on these pages come from this double set of lantern slides produced in the late 1880s. Individually hand coloured onto the glass plates, these images capture the Western Isles and their way of life in evocative detail. Published here for the first time as a complete set, many of the images, particularly those of St Kilda and its inhabitants, are iconic and well known among enthusiasts of Western Isles history. However, these contemporary hand coloured slides are rarely seen and present a new light on life in the Western Isles, produced as they were fifty years before colour photography came to Scotland.

The photographs were taken by the Aberdeen photographers George Washington Wilson (GWW) and Norman MacLeod of Aberdeen when they travelled through the Western Isles to St Kilda in 1886. It was customary for GWW to label all the images with his company trade mark "G.W.W.". As a consequence, MacLeod is virtually unknown and for over 100 years his images have been credited to George Washington Wilson himself, even though Wilson never travelled to St Kilda.

The GWW Company

George Washington Wilson (1823–1893) was the second son of a soldier turned Banffshire crofter[1]. He left school at the age of twelve and was apprenticed to a carpenter and house painter, but in 1841 travelled to Edinburgh to study drawing and painting, being described as a 'young and rising artist'[2]. Returning to Aberdeen in 1849 after trips to London and Paris, he set up as a portrait miniaturist and supplemented his income by teaching drawing and painting. In 1852, he equipped himself with a photographic studio and moved into a short-term partnership with John Hay, resulting in a special prize for the excellence of their 'Collodio-Calotype Portraits' in the Aberdeen Exhibition of 1853.

Wilson was only one of many to take up commercial photography in the 1850s but he brought an entrepreneurial flair to the business together with great artistic and technical skill. Wilson was never just a 'taker of pictures' but always considered himself an 'artist and photographer'. His sense of composition was superb and, often including figures in the foreground to add a sense of proportion, he never lost his portrait artist's talent for lighting and proportion. In the 1860s and 1870s, Wilson travelled extensively across the length and breadth of Scotland and into England and Ireland, even visiting Egypt in 1878. He advertised widely in both general guidebooks like 'Black's Picturesque Tourist in Scotland' and specialist publications, such as J Watson Lyall's 'Sportsman's Guide'[3]. In turn Wilson's photographs were sought by authors and publishers for prestigious guide books such as MacBrayne's 'Summer Tours in Scotland' or Caledonian Railways 'Through Scotland'.

The firm's 1863 catalogue listed four hundred and seventy three Stereoscopic and Album views, including English Cathedrals and Shipping. Wilson concentrated on the then established Scottish tourist centres of Iona, the Trossachs, Deeside, Edinburgh and Melrose. From his earliest days in business, he was associated with the tourist business and understood the powerful marketing benefits of the travel narrative. By 1877, the catalogue had grown to over four and a half thousand views with over one hundred and forty of Edinburgh alone. Prints were available in several sizes, plain or coloured, individually or in albums and as lantern slides.

As the business grew, Wilson trained other photographers to increase capacity. His eldest son Charles was responsible for 1880s images of London and travelled to South Africa for images in the late 1890s. Robert Bevan, George Gellie (son of William Gellie, Wilson's early assistant) and Norman MacLeod all became photographers of note. MacLeod worked with Wilson on a Highland tour in 1885 and travelled to St Kilda in 1886 to take some of the firm's most iconic images of that Scottish outpost. One of the most senior photographers was Fred Hardie and it was he who was chosen to travel with Charles Wilson to South Africa and then on to Australia to take photographs for the company.

By the late 1880s, Wilson's sons were effectively running the business. The demand for views and stereoviews was declining and the sons worked hard to re-establish the business. One of their major efforts was focussed on lantern slides. The 1890s saw a significant increase in the range of slide sets offered, and their catalogue listed hundreds of sets available. While Scottish subjects still formed a major element, coverage extended throughout Europe to Russia, Canada, the United States, South America, Japan, Africa, New Zealand and, of course, Australia. Charles Wilson claimed that thousands of slides sold abroad as well as in Britain, 'especially to Germany and America'. In addition to the standard UK format of three and a quarter inches square, GWW produced lantern slides in the American three and a quarter inch by four inch format usually marked 'G.W.W.' but they also produced them labelled for American retailers, including "Specially Produced for T.H. McAllister of New York".

The catalogue also included humorous slide sets and the set 'Animal Locomotion', fifty-one slides taken from Professor Edward Muybridge's photographic studies of animal and human locomotion. There were also sets

1   Taylor, Roger. (1981) *George Washington Wilson, Artist and Photographer*. Aberdeen University Press, Aberdeen.

2   Durie, Alastair, J. 'Tourism and Commercial Photography in Victorian Scotland: The Rise and Fall of G.W.Wilson & Co., 1853-1908.' *Northern Scotland*, 12 (1992): pg 90.

3   Lyall, J. Watson. (1915) *Sportsman's Guide to the Rivers, Loch, Moors and Deer Forest of Scotland*. J. Watson Lyall & Co. London. 1915.

aimed at the Educational market. Some series were created from their own images, others were bought in[4], and occasionally, sets were made up for individuals using their own photographs. By the 1890s, they were also producing wall calendars and beginning to market postcards, which was to become their second major market after lantern slides.

Wilson died in 1893 after a long illness, possibly caused, or at least aggravated, by the early photographic chemicals he worked with. He left only £7,475, most of which went to support his widow and unmarried daughters and the business was short of finance. In 1893, the Lord Advocate in Aberdeen brought a case on behalf of the Inland Revenue against the Company for duty outstanding on the business. It was a long, drawn out legal case based on a fine point of law regarding duty payable when a business sold without payment of cash – the sons paid their father an annuity. The Inland Revenue were eager to establish this as a test case and eventually won after two months in court. The costs are unknown but must have been considerable. Consequently, the sons inherited a business with poor long-term viability.

The growth of lantern slide sales took the business from a loss of £1,196 in 1886-1887 to a profit of £3,349 in 1891. However, despite the son's efforts and notwithstanding the selling of various parts of the business and some buildings, they could not sustain things and the firm of George Washington Wilson and Co. went into liquidation in 1902. The name was retained for a new company, which continued to publish views, manufacture lantern slides and postcards. Nevertheless, concludes Roger Taylor, "there was a certain futility in whatever they attempted (and) they were almost bound to fail".[5] In July 1908, G.W. Wilson & Co. was wound up and the remaining assets sold off. Charles Wilson kept a small lantern slide business going in Aberdeen until 1913, when it was sold to the slide makers Newton & Co. of London.

John Milne Auctioneers of Aberdeen sold the entire stock of GWW in a three-day auction, on the 9th, 10th and 11th of July 1908. All 65,000 negative glass plates were offered in sixty six lots, county by county and country by country. The prices realized were ludicrously low, making a total of only £284, with some lots unsold. Fred Hardie purchased a large number of the plates and he continued to operate a postcard business until the 1920s. Eventually the plates sold again to local Aberdeen photographer, Archibald J. B. Strachan, who, on moving to new and smaller business premises in 1954, offered them to the Library of Aberdeen University, where, today, they form the basis of The George Washington Wilson Collection.

---

4   Apart from images of the more remote places or countries that company photographers could not cover, GWW also bought in photographs that were not considered standard company subjects. For example, Charles Reid of Wishaw, Scotland, supplied them with Animal Studies photographs for many years.

5   Taylor, Roger. (1981) George Washington Wilson, Artist and Photographer. Aberdeen University Press, Aberdeen.

From Oban to Skye — Original Introduction

To give anything like an exhaustive description of the Hebrides in a lecture such as this would be almost impossible, but since these Islands as well as their inhabitants have of late awakened considerable public interest, a few facts about them may not be out of place.

The people inhabiting the Islands called the Hebrides are in their habits and general make-up different from the Lowlanders of Scotland. This, doubtless, to a large degree has resulted, not only from the lack of friction and contact with the loyal, energetic, intelligent and practical Scotsman, but arises largely from the fact that at one time they were under the rule of the Norsemen or Sea Kings, and, though subsequently connected nominally with Scotland, were vassals to the Lords of the Isles, who for want of direct heirs eventually ceased to exist. But the two powerful houses of Macdonald and Macleod distributed themselves into petty chiefs who ruled autocratically as they willed; and since then, though these Islands have been bought and sold repeatedly, the object of the buyer usually seems to have been simply an investment for his personal profit, without any consideration as to the needs of the native poor people – who are huddled-up in the most rude, primitive, and uncomfortable surroundings. The barrenness of these Islands, as well as the people's loss of their individuality through oppression, keeps them poor and heartless.

The insecurity of their holdings also produces very undesirable results. The proprietor, with a stroke of his pen or by a word of his mouth, can turn out of their small possessions as many as he chooses, and convert miles on miles of their lands into deer forests or sheep runs for either pleasure or profit, according as whim or selfishness would seem to suggest.

Slide No: 1 – SOUND OF MULL. From the heights above the beautiful bay of Oban, on one of these lovely afternoons so peculiar to the West Coast, the prospect is truly magnificent. Before you the Sound of Mull sparkles in the sunlight, broken up here and there by the rocks on the west side of Kerrera, among which the Shepherd's Hat is a very prominent object. In the distance where the sky and water appear to meet, the mountains of Mull stand out boldly, while the clouds overhead show a variety of colour such as no hand can adequately portray. Beyond this beautiful prospect lie the comparatively unknown Islands of the Outer Hebrides.

Slide No: 2 – OBAN. Oban will be found a most convenient point to start from on board Mr. McBrayne's well-appointed steamers, so with the last bell and the steam whistle sounding in your ears, the steamer glides gaily along through Oban bay, passing Dunolly Castle on the right and Kerrera on the left, then enters the Sound of Mull. Still steaming on, you pass Duart Castle with its gloomy memories of the treacherous Maclean, while away on the Morven shore stands the remains of Ardtornish Castle, where at one time the Lords of the Isles held their rude parliaments and discussed ways and means for the subjugation of Scotland, which for them ended disastrously at the battle of Harlaw. The first place of importance we touch at is Tobermory.

Slide No: 3 – TOBERMORY. As the steamer enters the beautiful bay of Tobermory the little town with its half circle of white houses, backed by hill terraces, on which pretty villas are perched and flanked by sombre pine plantations, is a pleasant picture, and takes heart and eye at once. The steamer is usually detained here for a considerable time unloading cargo. This operation, however, becomes wearisome, and it is preferable to pay the landing tax and have a look around and see if on closer examination the town maintains its prepossessing character; if not, there are beautiful sylvan walks and waterfalls beyond the clatter of the steam crane and the shouting of Gaelic-speaking porters. After leaving Tobermory, the Ru-na-Gaul lighthouse is passed, and to the westward of this lies the Bloody Bay, where "Alastair Crotach" of Dunvegan, the hunchback son of William, chief of the Macleods, was slain in battle, in 1493. The next point of interest is Ardnamurchan point, or the Cape of the Great Seas, and the most westerly land of Great Britain, when on a breezy day the swell of the great Atlantic tests the seaworthiness of many a tourist. West from the point lies the low Island of Coll, to the northward Muke, with the peaked mountains of the Island of Rum, and the long wall of the Scuir of Eigg. Between the Islands of Eigg and Rum may be seen the many crests of the Coolin mountains of Skye.

Slide No: 4 – EIGG. The Isle of Eigg is the most remarkable looking Island in the British seas. The Scuir rises to a height of 1272 feet, and as seen from the deck of the steamer is very imposing. In this Island there is a remarkable cave, which was the scene of one of the most hideous atrocities narrated in Scottish annals. The entrance to this cave lies at the base of a cliff near the south-east shore of the Island, and barely admits of one person crawling through at a time. The cavern inside is both lofty and spacious, being 260 feet long, 27 feet broad, 20 feet high, and bears all the appearances of having been scooped out by the action of the sea. About 230 years since a party of Macleods from Skye landed on Eigg on a reiving expedition but were captured, tied, and sent adrift in their boat. They in return, nursing the hatred and revenge which were recognised virtues in the Celt, came back in force to put the natives of Eigg to the sword. They, however, fled to the Cave of Francais, and might have been perfectly secure, had not one of their number ventured out too soon in order to see what the enemy were about. He returned to the cave, and told the rest that the homesteads of Eigg had been given to the flames. The Macleods were at their boats, and about to return home, when they observed the Macdonald from the cave on the sky line of the Scuir; a slight shower of snow made it an easy matter to trace his footprints to the cave's mouth, at the entrance of which they piled up whatever would burn, and setting fire to it prevented the escape of the unfortunate inmates, who eventually succumbed to suffocation. It is recorded that 200 MacDonalds perished in that cave, and very recently there still remained 67 skeletons in it.

Slide No: 5 – ARMADALE CASTLE. After leaving Eigg the peaks of the Coolins stand out very clearly, and just before entering the Sound of Sleat the steamer makes a call opposite Armadale Castle, the residence of the lineal descendant of the Lord of the Isles – Lord Macdonald. This Castle is surrounded by plantations not surpassed by any in the country, and when through the openings of these really noble trees you obtain a glimpse of the Castle itself, a handsome, modern looking building rising from sweeps of closely shaven lawn, you find it hard to believe this is Skye, and that you are within a few miles northward, of a long stretch of moory desolation, while about a mile and a half distant, in an opposite direction, are a number of miserable crofters' homes, surrounded by very poor land, from which the tenants, with the aid of the crooked spade and such seaweed as they can carry from the shore, manage to raise a little oats and potatoes. Here, as at many other places of the steamer's calls, communication with the shore is maintained by ferry boats, under the care of Mr. McBrayne's agent, who is also the local time table and cyclopedia for all information in connection with the steamers. After leaving Oban, many calls are made in the same manner, namely, a boat is brought alongside before you are aware, and when made fast, a few Gaelic monosyllables are exchanged, then the clatter of the stream crane commences, and goes on, while boxes, barrels, bags of oats, meal, flour, and potatoes are tumbled into it in a most indiscriminate fashion until a stranger imagines the boat must sink. Suddenly a few human beings crowd the already apparently overloaded boat, and, after one or two Gaelic phrases are exchanged, the screw commences moving, and very soon the small boat and its load is left far behind to be rowed ashore.

Slide No: 6 – SKYE FROM BALMACARRA. Just before passing through the narrowest part of water between Skye and the mainland, the Coolin range comes into full view. On the Skye shore stands the shattered tower of Castle Moil, said to have been built by a Danish princess, and it is alleged she stretched a chain cable from shore to shore, so that no craft should pass without paying toll. After calling at Broadford, you skirt the Isle of Scalpay and enter the Sound of Raasay, sheltered on the south side by Marsgow and Ben Lee, this latter hill is now historically famous as being one of the bones of contention at the commencement of the present crofter agitation. Between these two hills Loch Sligachan runs inland for a considerable distance, and, as seen from the deck of the steamer, its waters appear to wash the base of the grandest of the black Coolin range – Scuir-na-Gillean.

Slide No: 7 – RAASAY HOUSE. On the opposite shore of the Sound is seen the beautiful mansion of Raasay House. The Island of Raasay was formerly the property of a Macleod, who acknowledged Macleod of Dunvegan as his chief.

Slide No: 8 – PORTREE. After proceeding a short distance up the Sound the steamer passes within the imposing headlands that guard the approach to Portree, i.e. the King's Port. The town, as seen from the pier, folds two irregular ranges of white houses, the one range rising steeply above the other, around a noble bay, the entrance to which is sheltered by rocky precipices. At a little distance the houses are as white as shells, and, as in summer they are set in the greenest of foliage, the effect is strikingly pretty.

At the pier the imperturbable character of the true Highlander may be noticed. The arrival of the steamer being the event of the day, most of those who have nothing particular to do congregate on the pier, and they would not unnaturally be expected to show some interest in this event; but no! the Highlander would as soon think of turning his back on his foe as of expressing astonishment at anything.

To the visitor the place does not seem specially remarkable, but everything is relative in this world, and Portree is the capital of Skye. The tourist seldom lingers long in the town, but within a short distance of it finds many subjects that, if not at all striking, are at least very interesting.

The crofter agitation having excited interest throughout the country without disseminating a corresponding amount of reliable information, a few remarks here regarding the crofters and their homes may be interesting.

Slide No: 9 – CROFTERS' DWELLINGS. Such a home savours a good deal of Robinson Crusoe life, but a taste of the Skye climate, with all its accompanying discomforts, would very speedily dissolve any enthusiasm for living in such a dwelling. The average dwelling in the West Highlands is not a model edifice, and is open to wind and always pervious to rain. An old bottomless herring firkin, stuck in the roof, usually serves for a chimney, but the blue peat reek disdains the aperture, and streams wilfully through the door and the "crannies" in the wall and roof. The interior is seldom well lighted. What light there is proceeding rather from the orange glow of the peat fire, on which a large pot is simmering, than from the narrow pane, with its great bottle green bulls-eye. The rafters, which support the roof, are black and glossy with soot. The sleeping accommodation is limited. The floor is the beaten earth; the furniture is scanty, there is hardly even a chair, stools and stones worn smooth by the usage of many generations have to do instead. The door usually opens into the byre, which is separated from the living room by a low partition, sufficient to keep "crummy" out, while fowls cluck about and assert their co-tenancy with the crofter and his family; the darkness of the outer apartment is impenetrable, excepting directly opposite the entrance, while outside there is usually a pool of stagnant odiferous liquid, in which one or two dirty ducks guddle.

Slide No: 10 – WASHING DAY. In such a dwelling, when in wet weather the rain percolates through the roof and falls in ominous black drops all around, it is not to be wondered at if cleanliness does not rank as a leading virtue; yet, when washing day comes round, there are some who do it thoroughly. Thus, a rude temporary fire-place is erected close by some running water, above this a huge pot is set, filled with water from the stream that runs close at hand, and very soon a couple of washers go through a good deal in a way it would be impossible to accomplish inside, even the best crofter's house in the Highlands.

Slide No: 11 – THE SPINNING WHEEL. The spinning wheel, once seen in every Highland hut, is not now so general, even in Skye, as in bygone days. Shops are more common now than ever they were, and good clothing can be had from factories far cheaper than they can be made "home-spun," provided there be any cash in hand.

In many cases the sheep, because of "inbreeding," are depreciating both in mutton and wool, and it is not unusual in the spring to see many of them miserably lean and almost naked. Nevertheless, there remains sufficient vitality in many cases to produce good wool, which the poor people spin, and weavers are seen in every township plying at the loom weaving the comfortable "home-made" garments for the people.

Slide No: 12 – OCTOGENERIANS. Life in the Highlands, notwithstanding the neglect of sanitary laws, is not so unhealthy after all, if we may judge by the number of old people to be seen going about. The two worthies, both over eighty years of age, and living at Fisherfield, Portree, are genuine specimens of true, noble, generous, and hospitable Highlanders; this latter trait is very noticeable among the old people, and, although they are shy towards strangers, any one who will take the trouble to become acquainted with them, and go in and out among them, will find much that is worth imitating.

The most important names in Skye are Macdonald and Macleod. Both are of great antiquity, and it is as difficult to discover the source of either in history as it is to discover the source of the Nile in the deserts of Central Africa. Macdonald is understood to be of pure Celtic origin. Macleod was originally a Norseman. Macdonald was the Lord of the Isles, and more than once crossed swords with the Scottish kings. The two families intermarried often, and quarrelled oftener. They put marriage rings on each other's fingers, and dirks into each other's hearts. Lord Macdonald had his modern castle at Armadale, while Macleod retains his old eyrie at Dunvegan with its drawbridge and dungeons.

Slide No: 13 – CORN GRINDING. This is a very old custom still existing in Skye: for the Isles man not only loves the place of his nativity, but clings to every custom that has been handed down by his forefathers. Although an old law so far back as the thirteenth century provided "That no man shall presume to grind his own grain," excepting in very peculiar circumstances, and more recently the laird could oblige his tenants to make use of the more expeditious methods of grinding, and empowered his miller "to search out and break any querns he can find," as machines that defraud him of the toll. The quantity of oats raised by a crofter in a good season is not large, and not infrequently as the result of an unfavourable season, or the ravages of deer, it is too insignificant to take to the mill. In such a case the "clach-cuaich" is brought into requisition. The grain is first thoroughly dried in a pot over a peat fire; then the mill being adjusted, the grain is dropped in at the opening in the middle of the upper stone with one hand, while the other revolves the upper stone by means of a very rude lever adjustment. The nether stone being slightly convex, and the lower surface of the upper stone being concave, the meal falls out all round on to a cloth spread out to receive it. In order to remove the outer husk it is sifted though a sieve, made by stretching a sheepskin on a frame, and then perforating it all over with a red hot iron. The old man in the picture holds a sieve of this description.

Slide No: 14 – THE "CAS CHROM". The method of cultivating the ground in the Hebrides, and in some parts of the Highland mainland, is no less primitive than grinding the corn; and a Highlander will tell you that the crooked spade is a certain indication of poverty. The ordinary croft of the Isles man is small, and often so steep and rocky that the use of a plough is out of the question, even if a crofter could possess and man one.

Yet a little more energetic cultivation, would in many cases bring its own reward, as the crooked spade, or "cas chrom," only turns the surface of the soil; and the crofter's plot being so small the same ground is turned over year after year, the result being a very poor return of oats or potatoes, the former is often never matured, or it may be devoured by the proprietor's game, while the latter is not infrequently frosted. The haste and hurry of the nineteenth century has not taken hold of the Isles men yet, for they take everything very easily, and even in the spring of the year, when they may be said to be very busy getting the "croft" ready for seed. It is unusual for them to commence working until three or three-and-a-half hours after sunrise, but to give them all credit, they will work as long as they can see.

Slide No: 15 – CROFTER AND DAUGHTER. In some instances, when the soil is soft, the help of a spade is often necessary in order to turn the full length of the blade, as in the case of the crofter and his daughter planting potatoes.

Slide No: 16 – GIRL WITH CREEL. The women in the Highlands do a heavy share of the labour in the spring, by carrying in creels of sea weed, which is almost their only manure. Most of their cattle graze out all the year round; besides they are not careful to look after the cattle droppings, which a practical husbandman considers very valuable. Consequently the sea weed is valuable as a fertilizer throughout the Hebrides. Certain portions of the inshore are set apart for particular districts, these are shorn at regular intervals; while on the west side of the Islands large quantities of sea weed can be gathered after a storm, and women may be seen climbing up very steep precipices, with loads enough for a horse, and it is peculiarly noticeable that, when a man engages in this work, he leads a horse with panniers attached, and filling these with sea weed, the crofter marches by the animal's side, with his hands in his pockets to keep them warm.

Slide No: 17 – STORR ROCK. Among places of interest accessible from Portree, the "Old Man" of Storr is the most important. It is easily seen on a clear day from the wooded knoll above the pier, unless it should happen to be enveloped in a night-cap of mist. There is no regular road to it, and in fine weather tourists often take the most direct route, that is a straight road in a northerly direction along the ridge of the hill that gradually rises from Portree in the direction of the "Old Man." The road chosen for the ponies is very tortuous, as so many bogs have to be avoided.

The "Old Man" of Storr, a pinnacle 160 feet high rises from the eastern slope of the Storr. Cliffs and pinnacles repeat the wonders of the Quiraing on a vaster scale, and the mimicry of a ruined city is re-produced, and wonderfully realised by the presence of clouds on the hill. Approaching the mountain top from the north, the ascent is so gradual that the stranger is brought to a sudden standstill, by finding the ground beneath him suddenly cut down for 500 feet; and, on looking around, the dissevered rock is seen piled up in the most fantastic forms, while the "Old Man" stands alone, as if keeping watch over the ruins.

Slide No: 18 – PRINCE CHARLIE'S CAVE. The Storr Rock can be reached by a small boat from Portree in fine weather, and this route is usually taken by those who wish to see Prince Charlie's Cave. The cavern is screened by plants and stalactites, and on entering it is found wet and dismal. An inner chamber somewhat raised above the outer afforded Prince Charlie shelter, and is the immediate background of the famous picture painted by Thomas Duncan of the "Prince in hiding" attended by Flora Macdonald.

Slide No: 19 – SLIGACHAN HOTEL AND MARSGOW. From Portree, Glen Sligachan, Scuir-na-gillean, and Loch Coruisk may be visited, and Sligachan Hotel is usually made the starting point for those places. The Hotel stands alone at the entrance of this wild glen, and is distant from Portree about 9½ miles. Shortly after leaving Portree, on looking back, the Storr Rock is seen to recede during the first half of the journey, while directly in front the Coolin range becomes more and more imposing as you near the Hotel, which stands under the shadow of Scuir-na-gillean, the grandest of the black Coolin range.

Slide No: 20 – SCUIR-NA-GILLEAN, from SLIGACHAN BRIDGE. From the Hotel the favourite walk is along the glen to Loch Coruisk. About midway through Glen Sligachan you skirt the base of Marsgow, that huge and isolated red Coolin – contrasting very strikingly with the black and rugged outline of Scuir-na-gillean that bounds the glen on your right.   Round the eastern flank of the Scuir is the deep gorge of the Hart o' Corrie, running into the depths of the black Coolins, and leading to the Loat o' Corrie – a stony abyss on the S.W. face of Scuir-na-gillean, described as perfectly terrible in its grimness. Down this deep gorge runs the Sligachan burn, a stream whose marvellous transparency seems to impart a brilliancy to the well-worn stones of various colours that form its bed, such as no mosaic work could possibly surpass.

Slide No: 21 – BLAVEN. After clearing the base of Marsgow, Blaven rises like a huge wall without break or space. From the track (for road it cannot be called), a magnificent view of this very striking mountain can be had just before beginning to ascend Drumhain, from which the weird-looking peaks of the entire Coolin range appear to pass through all fantastic forms, while clouds rest on the black crevices on their sides. Over these mountains the eagle may yet be seen hovering, and from them ravens fly all the way to Rum to work havoc among the sheep. The descent from Drumhain to the shore of Loch Coruisk must be made very carefully, as the slope is steep, and a false step might land one at the bottom sooner than in the circumstances would be convenient.

Slide No: 22 – LOCH CORUISK. Here we have one of the most savage scenes of desolation in Britain. Loch Coruisk, meaning in Gaelic "The Kettle of Water", not at all an inapt description; conceive a large lake filled with dark green water, girt with torn and shattered precipices, the bases of which are strewn with ruin since an earthquake passed that way, and whose summits jag the sky with grisly splinter and peak. There is no motion here, save the white vapour streaming from the abyss and curling round the peaks that still bear traces of the winter snow. The utter silence weighs like a burden, for excepting the ripple of the waves on the shores of Loch Scavaig, or the croak of the raven soaring far overhead, there is nothing to break the stillness. The whole scene is one of terrible barrenness and solitude. Here the eagle survives unmolested, and may be seen spreading his wings majestically almost any day. The lake is but a few feet above sea level, into which

> "A wild stream with headlong shock
> Comes brawling down a bed of rock
> To mingle with the main!"
> - Scott

To ascend is a much more difficult task, and, as you must of necessity pick your way over huge boulders, well worn stones, and bogs, it should be done very leisurely, so as to allow of time to enjoy the view to be got of –

Slide No: 23 – LOCH SCAVAIG. Sparking beautifully in the afternoon sun; while the sharp hills of Rum stand out boldly where sky and sea appear to meet. When the top is reached the view of the whole Coolin range is very grand. Rising from the western shore of Loch Scavaig is Garsven, and from this peak, towards the north-east, rise peak after peak of every variety of form and name till from the northern shoulder of the last hill runs the picturesque crest of the Scuir-na-gillean rising into a remarkable pinnacle of 3,220 feet, this ends the range of the black Coolins.

Slide No: 24 – MACLEOD'S MAIDENS. The coast line, westward, is very rugged and the cliffs at Talisker Head are the highest on the coast of Skye rising perpendicularly from the sea.

Further west are "Macleod's Maidens", three remarkable rocky spires rising sheer out of the water, shaped like women, around whose feet the foamy wreaths are continually forming, fleeting, and disappearing. Formerly there were four, but the furthest out maiden has succumbed to the continuous action of the waves. They are pointed out by the natives as the mother and her two daughters.

Slide No: 25 – WATERSTEIN POINT. Continuing in a north-westerly direction you come on Waterstein Point, a rugged headland rising to a great height, and famous as being the debatable ground where more recent land law agitation commenced. Among these rugged and inaccessible cliffs hawks, ravens, and sea eagles, defy the boldest adventurer and rear their young in perfect security. After leaving the rugged coast line and joining the road that leads to Dunvegan, we pass through a very extensive crofting district. This is the famous "Glendale", where, during the spring months, you may study with interest the very antiquated method of tilling the ground in the islands. Even on the mainland the same custom prevails when the crofts are small and the people poor, but it is universal all over the Western Isles.

Continuing the journey, Loch Dunvegan soon comes into view. At its head stands the very ancient Castle of Dunvegan, and for many a mile round everything reminds you that the country is Macleod's.

Slide No: 26 – DUNVEGAN CASTLE. Dunvegan Castle is supposed to be the oldest inhabited house in Scotland, one portion of it is said to have been built in the ninth century. The old part of the castle looks towards the sea, and the only entrance at one time was by a flight of steps leading through a narrow archway, up which perhaps came Macleod of Harris after he sank the barge of his father-in-law in the misty Minch. One of the towers of the castle was built by Alexander the Hunchbacked, the son of William, slain at the battle of Bloody Bay, near Tobermory, in 1493. In this castle is preserved an ox horn mounted with silver rim, holding about five imperial pints, said to be the drinking horn of "Rory More" i.e., Big Roderick, who was knighted by James VI. To empty this horn at a drink was considered a necessary feat to be performed by the chief of Macleod on coming of age, but a false bottom has lessened its capacity for modern appetites. The Macleods, like other chiefs, have a ghost which haunts one of the chambers of Dunvegan. Many a strange tale is also told of the days when the rival chiefs, Macleod and Macdonald, were watching for an opportunity to do each other mortal injury, as how Donald Gorm, after seeking shelter in the castle one stormy night, defied Macleod at dinner and proudly told him that wherever Macdonald of Sleat sits is the head of the table. That night, however, he narrowly escaped being burned in the barn through Macleod's treachery, and next morning, with his bodyguard of twelve men, marched down to where his barge was moored with his piper playing in front, to the astonishment of all in the castle.

Slide No: 27 – UIG BAY. Crossing the country from Dunvegan in an easterly direction, you join the main road that skirts the shores of Loch Snizort leading to Uig, with its beautiful bay, which lies like a horse shoe, with a belt of brown shore and cultivated fields, and a mountain terrace for a background. On the north shore of Uig Bay is a high waterfall, and at the north headland of the bay is a basalt ridge, from which the deep green sward runs with a smooth slope to the sea. The anchorage in Uig Bay suffers from heavy seas in strong northwest winds. After seeing the iron bound coasts of Skye, the truth of Pennant's description of Uig will not be disputed. He speaks of it as "a fertile bottom laughing with corn!"

Slide No: 28 – QUIRAING. The special point of interest near Uig is the Quiraing, distant six miles over a very rough road, the last mile being a steep mountain path. At the entrance to the Quiraing is the "Needle", a pinnacle 120 feet high, past which the path runs up to the grassy plateau, called the Quiraing, the origin of which name is unknown. This grassy space, large enough to parade a regiment, is on the table-like surface of a rock having around it a confusion of pinnacles, spires, and fantastic crags. These assume grotesque resemblance to shattered towns, and when partly hidden by mist and rain suggest a chaos of weird and colossal masonry. The Quiraing, like the Coolins, defies description; nothing yet written conveys a worthy description of the features of either. Through breaks in the cliffs, magnificent glimpses of the scenery of Loch Staffin – a bay immediately beneath the Quiraing are caught. The isles of Rona and Raasay, besides an extensive stretch of the mainland are seen if the day is fine. The Scour More, on the slope of which the crags of the Quiraing lie scattered, rises 1774 feet above the sea, and all along its eastern face basalt cliffs are strewn. From the sea these shattered cliffs appear like the wreck of a great city, and present the most wonderful scenic effects.

Slide No: 29 – KILT ROCK. Between Steinsholl Inn on Loch Staffin and the Ru-na-Barin the coast line presents ranges of basalt cliffs, in which the pillars are more slender and much higher than in the Island of Staffa. Along the top of these columns strata run horizontally, giving the appearance of buildings in which shattered pillars and broken pediments constantly recur.

Slide No: 30 – DUNTULM CASTLE. Nine miles from Uig is Duntulm Castle, and one way to it leads over a long slope of agricultural land called "the garden of Skye". On the verge of Loch Snizort the stack of Scudburgh is seen standing like a lighthouse. Duntulm Castle, originally the site of a "dun", once the stronghold of pirate Norsemen, anterior to the Norwegian invasion in the reign of Harold Harfager. It is a considerable ruin, perched upon a precipitous cliff, and has still an imposing look. The castle built by the chiefs of Clan Donnel in the twelfth century, remained the home of the Macdonalds till they removed to Mugstadt. "Big-Donald-with-the-blue-eyes", Lord of the Isles and grandson of Donald Gorm, who lost his life besieging Eilan-donan Castle in Loch Duich, at one time starved a kinsman to death in the dungeon of Duntulm. This kinsman having conspired against his uncle, wrote to an accomplice in Skye, and by the same opportunity sent a friendly letter to Donald Gorm, but in transit the letters passed into the hands of one who could not read, and this person handed to Donald Gorm the one that revealed his nephew's treachery. He was immediately captured, carried to Skye, and immured in Duntulm; there he was starved to death, after first being supplied with a liberal meal of salt food, and daily after this to mock his thirst, a covered drinking cup was lowered to him, which on being uncovered, was found empty.

Slide No: 31 – FLORA MACDONALD'S TOMBSTONE. Near by is Kilmuir churchyard, where reposes the dust of the heroine of the West Highlands, Flora Macdonald. For a long period this interesting spot was sadly neglected, and the insatiable tourist might with impunity carry away a chipping of the tombstone, or pluck a souvenir from the nettles that flourished perennially o'er her grave. More recently a cross was erected, which in turn yielded to the force of the storm and was broken, but this has been replaced by another that still stands. Looking across the Minch from the cliffs at Duntulm Castle, Harris, as well as the low-lying island of North Uist, are distinctly visible on a fine day. On South Uist the site of Flora Macdonald's birthplace is pointed out; and in order to hear some of the thrilling tales of the "forty-five" narrated by a Highlander, or see a few of the places associated with Bonnie Prince Charlie, be sure and visit the Outer Hebrides.

The Outer Hebrides — Original Introduction

The Outer Hebrides, including that large and elongated group of Islands, extending from the Butt of Lewis on the north to Barra on the south, are, when viewed on the map, suggestive of one island partially recovered from submersion. This is most noticeable from North Uist southward where the land, besides being very little elevated above sea level, is indented by a great number of lochs – the result being a coast line very much out of proportion to the superficial area.

The low lying islands usually present more verdure than is to be met with on the more elevated Long Island; but, altogether they contrast very strikingly with Skye, where nature appears in its wildest and most romantic features.

Social life is very much alike all over the Western Highlands, even to St Kilda, and it need not be surprising, if in many things, the Isles-men are behind their more fortunate countrymen in the Lowlands of Scotland, who were settled down peacefully to habits of industry long before the feudal system was broken up. While this continued, the natives of the West Highlands were only serfs; and it was not until the middle of the eighteenth century, when hereditary jurisdictions were done away with, that serfdom received its deathblow.

Since then, the attachment and mutual interest that at one time existed between the lairds and the people, have in many cases changed into distrust and hatred – chiefly on account of the frequency with which small Highland estates change hands, and partly on account of the inability of these islands to afford anything like a permanent remunerative industry, since the protective duties under which the manufacture of kelp was carried on, have been removed.

In the following Lecture, the most interesting subjects to be met with in a tour through the Hebrides are described; while the features of social and domestic life detailed, are such as any one visiting these islands may see.

Slide No: 32 – STORNOWAY. The Long Island, which we first proceed to visit after leaving Skye, is the most important of the Outer Hebrides. It is divided into two districts, Lewis and Harris, the former attached to Ross-shire and the latter to Inverness. The principal seaport and town on the Island is Stornoway, a very important place during the herring fishing season. The country everywhere in Lewis, excepting along the margin of the sea and in the immediate neighbourhood of Stornoway, is open, brown, bare, and quite uninteresting. As is usual in all the Islands of the Hebrides, there is a green line around the sea shore; but throughout the interior it is uninviting, and bare of everything almost of heath itself, although in early times it is said the Island was famed for its fertility.

Slide No: 33 – "DUNE" OF CARLOWAY. The "Dune" of Carloway is one of the few interesting subjects in Lewis, and is similar to remains throughout the country associated with the Picts.

The crofter's house in the foreground shows an average dwelling in point of architecture, for here, as throughout the Hebrides, their houses when made of stone are built without lime, and of very thick walls. The roof of bracken thatch rests on the top of the walls, leaving a foot or more of the wall-head uncovered. Were this not done, the gale of wind would get under the eaves and lift the roof away. Many heather ropes hold down the thatch, their ends being made fast to stones a foot or more square, which lie along the top of the walls.

Slide No: 34 – CIRCLE OF CALLERNISH. At the head of one of the inlets in Loch Bernera is a megalithic, cruciform, Druidical circle, called the Circle of Callernish. This Druidical temple is one of the largest, as well as the most complete of its kind in Scotland. The total number of stones, when the temple was complete, was sixty five, of which about forty five are still standing, ranging from sixteen to four feet in height.

In the immediate neighbourhood are several smaller circles, some of them, however, being as large as fifty feet in diameter. The circle occupies a striking position in an open track of moor, and appears to have been surrounded at a small distance by a trench or ditch, which is now in many places obscured, the same as at Stenneshouse, Orkney, and Stonehenge, England. It is thought by some that these circles may have been places of worship, erected by the Norsemen, as in some of the Northern Sagas; the temple of Thor is described as a circular range of upright stones, containing a central stone, called the stone of Thor, where the sacrifices or executions were performed.

Slide No: 35 – WEST LOCH TARBET. Leaving Loch Bernera and its cromlechs behind, and passing the boundary that separates Lewis from Harris, the next opening on the coast is West Loch Tarbet, a very deep indentation, and separated from the East Loch of the same name by a very narrow neck of land. The navigation of both these lochs is rendered very intricate by rocks and islands. A more joyless desert could not be well imagined than a general view of the Long Island while the mountainous part displays a greater extent of bare rock and black bog than is, perhaps, to be seen anywhere in Scotland.

Slide No: 36 – SCALPAY LIGHTHOUSE. Sheltering East Loch Tarbet from the N.E. winds is the Island of Scalpay, on which is erected a substantial lighthouse to guide the mariner.

In Harris considerable attention is given to wool-growing, and the name of this part of the Island has for a long time been attached to a particular kind of tweed manufactured there. Every branch of this particular industry is carried out entirely on the home principle, and in their dismal ill lighted huts the sound of the shuttle, etc. may be heard daily.

Slide No: 37 – WOOL WASHING. The subject shows their manner of washing the wool in process of preparation for spinning.

Slide No: 38 – RODEL CHURCH. The Hebrides are not particularly rich in ecclesiastical remains, and the church at Rodel is the only Pre-reformation church which still remains entire. The building is as curious as its history is obscure; the west front being distinguished by some extraordinary sculptures.

Slide No: 39 – A CROFT. The crofts throughout these Islands are very poor in soil, and quite insufficient for the maintenance of the people. The kelp industry, in which both old and young engage, helps considerably, but the people don't reap the remuneration from this they might, because they are obliged to leave the shipping of it to the "factor", who, while kelp is selling at £3 10s per ton, credits the people only with £2 per ton. This balance being considered necessary to recoup his trouble and risk, which on a sloop load amounts to a handsome sum. The crofters' houses in North Uist are scattered along the shores of the numerous lochs that intersect the Island, and, while these primitive dwellings look very romantic on a fine summer day, it is quite a different thing to have to spend twelve months a year in one of them, make a living, and pay rent for it besides.

Slide No: 40 – A TOWNSHIP – BORVE. The taxman, who usually holds the best of the land for grazing purposes, is not looked upon with favour by the people, as many of them have been removed from his more fertile ground to make room for his flocks, and they themselves compelled to settle down in a township, of which Borve is a very good specimen. Then they severally hold a little land, on which they do their best to raise oats and potatoes, while they also hold in common with their neighbours a stretch of hill ground or bog for grazing. But in some townships on the mainland the poor people dare not keep a cow, or even a pet lamb, lest the landlord's game or tax-man's sheep should be disturbed. The cattle throughout the Isles are generally lean, and in the springtime of a late season most pitiable; and the very little people can earn at the fishing is quite out of proportion to the tear, wear, and dangers to which they are exposed from the very frequent and tempestuous storms that come from the west.

Slide No: 41 – GENERAL VIEW. Across the Sound of Harris lies North Uist, a general view of which as seen from Ben Lee, contrasts very strikingly with the Long Island, for in North Uist the low, dark, half submerged land is intersected with narrow arms of the sea in every direction; indeed so intricate are these channels, that a stranger with a small boat would lose himself in the tortuous and canal-like labyrinths they form. On the shores of these narrow, river-like fiords, through which the tide ebbs and flows, dusky people gather wraick to burn for kelp.

Slide No: 42 – NORTH FORD. South of North Uist, and separated from it by what is called the North Ford, lies the Island of Benbecula. The distance between the Islands is four miles, and on certain days numbers of men, women, and children may be seen hurrying across the wet sands at low water. It is considered perilous to deviate from the recognised track, as at spring tides and with certain winds the flood may overtake those unacquainted. On these extensive stretches of sand, and all around the coast, large quantities of shell fish are gathered, and sent to the southern markets, for which the poor people receive a very small return; for by far the greater portion of it is swallowed up in rates for transit and commission on sales.

Slide No: 43 – WELL-TO-DO CROFTER'S HOUSE. The Island of Benbecula has nothing very striking about it, as it rises very little above sea level, and has only one low hill; but a great many fresh water lochs are scattered along its western coast, the Islands in these being a favourite resort for sea-birds. The Island formerly belonged to a branch of the Clanranalds, now it is the property of Lady Gordon Cathcart; and the crofters on this estate compare favourably with any throughout the Hebrides. The subject is a very snug crofter's dwelling.

Slide No: 44 – SOUTH FORD. The distance between Benbecula and South Uist is only about half a mile, which like the North Ford, is a stretch of wet sand at low water. The eastern coast is mountainous and cleft with Lochs Boisdale, Eynort and Skiport. This Island is considerably larger than North Uist, and consequently the industries in which the people engage are more varied.

Slide No: 45 – LOCH BOISDALE. Besides kelp making, at which old and young join, there is lobster fishing, and Loch Boisdale is often the scene of all bustle and excitement accompanying a good herring season.

No: 46 – KELP MAKERS. The kelp industry of the Hebrides is not so important now as it was some years ago. Yet the making of it is one of the chief occupations of a very large number of the inhabitants of these Islands, as usually the factor accepts it in payment for rent; the proprietors as a rule claim a heavy royalty on every ton of it manufactured, besides the rent charged by them for the crofts etc. The Duke of Argyle is no exception to this order of things. In the manufacture of this staple industry, many of the poor creatures have to leave home and dwell in huts partly dug into the earth and partly built of sod. In these they exist rather than live, while they are preparing the seasons necessary quantity of this material. The process of making it consists in gathering, drying and burning the sea weed, the residue constitutes the kelp.

Slide No: 47 – LOBSTER FISHER'S HUT. Another mode of living is by lobster fishing, and, during the summer, they pursue this on the west side of the Island, unless prevented by stormy weather; but in the wintry months the lobsters retire into deep water, or migrate to more sheltered ground on the east side of the Island, and in order to catch them, the fishermen have to leave their poor homes, and eke out a most miserable existence, similar to the kelp makers.

Slide No: 48 – A POORHOUSE. For the helpless aged there are provided wretched huts, mere apologies for a poorhouse. These are partly burrowed into the earth, and thus utilized. There the poor creatures must live or die on the shameful pittance of 2s. 6d. per month, and how they manage to exist on this is more than the writer of this paragraph can divine.

Slide No: 49 – PRINCE CHARLIE'S LANDING. This Island more than any of the others is associated with the forlorn days of "Bonnie Prince Charlie". To the south, and separated by a sound of half a mile, lies the small Island of Eriskay, where he landed for a very short time from the frigate "Doutelle", on his way to Scotland claiming its crown, which he conceived to be his right. Within a year he is back again with blasted hopes. After the battle of Culloden, having managed to make his way to the West Coast in safety, he embarked for the Long Island. Contrary winds, storms, and disappointments of several sorts, attended with hardships to which he could be little accustomed, drove him from place to place in that Island and its vicinity, till he gained South Uist, where he was received by Clan Ranald, who remained faithful to him in his distresses. But the unswerving fidelity of a faithful few, his safety was impossible, as search parties after having gone as far as St. Kilda looking for him, now landed on South Uist, and augmented the clans Macdonald and Macleod, who, though but a short time before stood aloof, were now fairly against the unfortunate Prince. With two thousand men searching with eagerness the interior of the Island, and its shores surrounded with small vessels of war, armed boats, and the like, escape seemed impossible; and it is not to be wondered at that he should resort to the wild slope of Ben More for shelter, and hide himself in its dark, rocky recesses.

Slide No: 50 – RUINS OF CLAN RANALD'S CASTLE.

Slide No: 51 – PRINCE CHARLIE'S CAVE. It was while in such extremities that the eager spirit of a noble minded woman received him, when, probably, every other means must have failed. Flora Macdonald, a relative of the Clan Ranald family, was on a visit to that chief's house at this period. Her stepfather was one of the Macdonalds of Sleat, and an enemy to the Prince's cause. In spite of her stepfather's hostility, she maintained that noble character so notable among the Highlanders, by planning and carrying out a scheme for the Prince's rescue. She started with the object of her devotion, playing the part of a female servant, and her presence of mind never left her, although more than once the awkwardness of the Prince in managing his petticoats nearly betrayed him.

Slide No: 52 – FLORA'S BIRTH PLACE. For her share in the Prince's escape she was imprisoned a short time, and, on being released, was married to Allan Macdonald of Kingsburgh, in whose house the Prince slept for a few hours. The latter part of her life she spent quietly in Skye, where she died in 1790; and at her special request, the sheets used by the Prince, during his short repose at Kingsburgh, did service as her winding sheet – they never having been put to any meaner offices, but had been carefully wrapped up by the lady of the house since that memorable night.

Slide No: 53 – CASTLE BAY. The Island of Barra is separated from South Uist by the Sound of Barra, full of rocks and shoals. At the southern end of the Island is the land-locked harbour of Castle Bay, at which steamers regularly call. When herring shoals are off the coast, the whole place resounds with stir, the air is laden with the odour of decaying fish, and the village of Castle Bay is thronged with the fishermen of the fleet.

Slide No: 54 – HERRING FLEET.

Slide No: 55 – KIESSIMULL CASTLE. The imposing ruin of Kiessimull Castle was at one time the stronghold of the Macneill of Barra, who is said to have entertained a very high opinion of his own importance. From the top of the highest tower of the castle it was the custom for a herald to announce the fact of the great Macneill having dined, and that all other potentates were at liberty to commence. One of the same Macneills having committed an act of piracy on an English vessel was captured by strategy and carried to Edinburgh; when tried there, he excused himself to James VI, by explaining that he wished to revenge the death of his mother, Queen Mary; this characteristic reply is said to have resulted in his release.

Slide No: 56 – SEA BIRDS' HOME. Throughout these Islands, on the numerous Islets that stud the lochs, myriads of sea birds rear their broods in peace, and lend an endless interest to their shores; but on the cliffs around Barra head, and on the detached isles south of it, they are so numerous that every ledge seems alive. Here they rear their young in perfect safety, since the old custom of bringing quantities of their eggs to Greenock for sale has been given up, as the steamers bring to the Island every necessity.

Slide No: 57 – St. KILDA AND STACK LEE. In a N.N. Westerly direction lies the Island of St. Kilda, the most remote and probably the most inaccessible of the British Isles. It is sixty miles west from the mainland of Lewis, and one hundred and forty miles from the nearest point of the mainland of Scotland. Excursions are sometimes made in the summer time by the steamers that regularly run to Loch Maddy and North Uist, but they are rare and uncertain. St. Kilda, so isolated from the outer world, is situated in the lonely expanse of the North Atlantic, and though not sufficiently elevated to form a picturesque object in mid-ocean, there is something in the very name of St. Kilda that excites expectation.

The Island is about three miles long and at the broadest part nearly two. On the southeast side there is a bay about half a mile in breadth and depth, the land descending to it by a steep declivity and terminating at one point in a stony and sandy beach, and at another in those low shelving rocks which form the landing place near to which the town is situated.

Slide No: 58 – TOWN AND BAY. The language here is the same as throughout the Western Isles, and in many respects the habits of the natives are like their nearest neighbours, but as vegetation on the Island is very meagre they find their subsistence in a manner quite different from them. Instead of using the crooked spade, and in return receiving a miserable crop of potatoes and oats, you will find through the aid of the hair rope combined with their unparalleled agility in scaling the precipitous cliffs, thousands of Fulmar are secured and salted down for the season's use. Then they have sheep in abundance pasturing on –

Slide No: 59 – BORERAY. Boreray, a small Island four miles distance from St. Kilda, and completely mantled in green with the exception of a margin around its base.

St. Kilda belongs to Macleod of Macleod, whose agent visits it twice a year to collect the rents, and supply the people with stores in return for feathers and oil from the Fulmar, which, with the wool they grow, constitutes the only source of wealth the St. Kildean's possess. Being so isolated it is not to be wondered at if in many things they are behind the age, and the occasional tourist who would treat them as they would South Sea Islanders gets a poor reception, but one who lives amongst them for a time will find them hospitable and trustworthy, and, like all Western Highlanders, they are very superstitious. They also wear an extraordinary load of flannel clothing, and declare that the arrival of a stranger gives them a cold.

Slide No: 60 – PARLIAMENT. Being beyond the reach of the laws that govern this realm they make their own laws. The solitary minister on the Island may advise in certain matters, and certainly has a limited influence, but it is their Parliament that fixes matters beyond appeal, and no stranger dare take part in its deliberations.

This Parliament meets daily, discusses the weather and state of the sea etc. etc., in a few Gaelic phrases; and by a majority the order of the day is fixed, and no single individual takes it upon himself to arrange his own business until after they unitedly decide what is best.

Slide No: 61 – HUNTING THE FULMAR. The great event of the season is the securing of the Fulmar, a bird as far as the British Isles are concerned is associated with St. Kilda only, and of the myriads of birds that live and rear their young on and around the Island they are most valuable to the natives. They are in the habit of securing them just before the young are able to fly; and in doing this considerable dexterity is necessary, as if the birds are surprised and not secured and strangled by the first clutch of the hand they immediately vomit on the intruder what a St Kildean prizes highly, namely, its oil. This they take from the bird at a more convenient time, and secure in bladders made of intestines taken from the Gannet which abounds on their Island.

Slide No: 62 – GANNETS' NESTS. They also use largely as an article of food wild fowls' eggs, many of these egg shells they preserve and sell to the insatiable tourist, who occasionally visits this very remote Island.

The men of St. Kilda are very nimble at the extremely hazardous occupation of rock climbing, and accidents are rare indeed; but if any should chance to fall they entertain a strange superstitious aversion to making any search for the remains; death being in the circumstances considered certain.

Slide No: 63 – WEST SIDE OF ST. KILDA. On the west side of the Island the cliffs are very grand, and it is amazing how they manage to secure the birds from spots apparently so inaccessible. The rocks on which the bird's nest are portioned off to each family a part – as although it is the custom to work for the common good, some families, in which there are several active grown up sons, prefer working independently of the community, and abide by their own lot. But excepting in a case of this kind it is impossible, the birds being often so difficult to get at, it is important that two or more climbers should be connected by their famous hair ropes, so that if one slips there is still a chance of those in the same connection remaining firm. The birds in many such cases are thrown over the cliffs into the sea to be picked up by a party in a boat.

Slide No: 64 – DIVIDING THE FULMAR. In bringing the birds together, either from the landing place or from more accessible parts, women and children join in helping, and it is considered degrading for the men to take any part in this. But two of the most respected aged men divide the birds, first they are divided into two heaps, the one including all the best birds, the second those not so good. They then proceed to divide them into as many lots as there are families in the Island – thus: a brace of birds from the best pile by one man, and a brace from the second best pile by the other man, and thrown into each lot until the whole are divided, the several portions being decided by lot – so that there can be no partiality.

Slide No: 65 – MAIDS AND MATRONS. The women of St. Kilda do all the work of carrying the fuel, and a man who would help his wife would at once be set down as showing a bad example. The number of women on the Island is slightly in excess of the men, and the population does not seem to increase, probably because of the great mortality among children, and as before they had a resident midwife only one in ten lived; now however the death rate is not nearly so high. Men as well as women knit, and having plenty of wool they spin and weave their own cloth, of which they have plenty for their own use, and the Macleod's factor at Dunvegan usually has a good supply of it for sale, he having received it as part payment of rent.

Slide No: 66 – GROUP WITH QUEEN. St. Kilda is not without its queen, who is said to be the best looking woman on the Island, and was first styled thus by a gentleman who visited the Island a good many years ago and spent some months among its natives with the view of reforming his habits. He is known to have won her affections, and she always on the arrival of a steamer makes inquiries regarding the faithless one. He, however, along with several others would do well to give St. Kilda a wide berth, as the natives have a significant way of enforcing their disapproval of anybody's misconduct.

Slide No: 67 – SUNSET ON THE ATLANTIC. Few indeed are the tourists who include St. Kilda in their programme of visitation, and such as try to do so may consider themselves fortunate, if on nearing its shores they find the weather favourable for landing, and when that is effected their visit must be very short, unless they are prepared to remain an indefinite period on shore. Then they may study the social economy of the St. Kildeans at their leisure, and watch the sunsets on the Atlantic with admiration.

The foregoing facts about the people of the lonely Island of St. Kilda may be interesting, and it may be added that no young man on the Island is considered eligible for marriage unless he possesses a rope sufficiently strong and satisfactory in every way for scaling the cliffs in search of the Fulmar, and the young woman to whom one of their famous ropes is bequeathed, ranks as rich and worth looking after with a view to matrimony.

The Origins and Development of the Magic Lantern

The magic lantern was the forerunner of today's slide projector. It is probable that the general form of the lantern was invented some time in the sixteenth century. The recognised configuration of light source, condenser, slide and focusing lens is attributed to Christian Huygens (1629 – 1695). In 1663 the London optician John Reeves started to make lanterns for sale. A Frenchman, Balthasar de Monconys recorded how he visited Reeves on the 17th May, 1663. "After we had eate, we went to Long Acre to see Mr. Reeves who makes telescopes. But he had none ready and deferred us to another time and also to show us how a bull's-eye lantern works." De Monconys then described the lantern. In his diary for August 19th, 1666, Samuel Pepys wrote, "Comes by agreement Mr Reeves bringing a lanthorn, with pictures in glass, to make strange things appear on a wall, very pretty". A later entry says how he purchased the lantern. The earliest recorded image of a magic lantern in a "modern" configuration was published in 1671 in Athanasius Kircher's "Ars Magna Lucis et Umbrae".

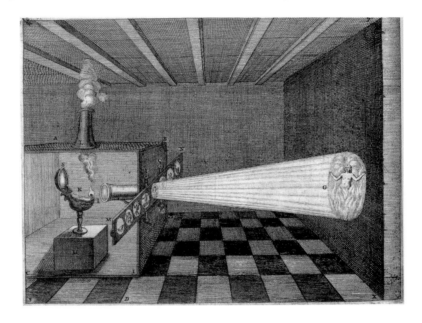

Illustration from Athanasius Kircher's "Ars Magna Lucis et Umbrae

This basic lantern configuration and hand painted images on hand made glass represented the general form of the magic lantern until the end of the 18th century. Using a light source of either candle or oil burner, the image was only bright enough to allow small groups to see the show. Itinerant lanternists travelled from town to town giving public entertainments for a small fee, while middle and upper class families held shows at home for family and friends.

In the 1780s Francois-Pierre-Ami Argand developed an oil burning lamp with a covering glass cylinder which gave a much brighter light. It was quickly adopted by a Frenchman, Etienne-Gaspard Robertson who developed a show with the lantern behind the screen, hidden from the audience. He also mounted the lantern on wheels and devised a focussing system linked to the turning of the wheels. With this device he could move the lantern towards or away from the screen, keeping the image in focus but changing its size. He specialised in what he termed "Phantasmagoria" or ghost shows, which were very popular in revolutionary Paris. He pioneered the concept of turning all the lights out in the theatre and accompanying his show with sound effects and music. By the end of the eighteenth century he was also projecting images onto smoke, giving them a 3D effect.

Early 19th Century Phantasmagoria Lantern

In 1825 Lieutenant Thomas Drummond developed a form of illumination known as limelight, based on an idea suggested in 1820 by Sir David Brewster. The limelight produced an intense white light by heating a piece of lime or calcium oxide with a flame of combined oxygen and hydrogen gases. Use of this light transformed not only the magic lantern but also the theatre, allowing spotlights to be used to pick out actors on stage ("to be in the limelight"). Its introduction allowed the lantern to project over a longer distance, allowing it to be used from the back of the theatre with large audiences.

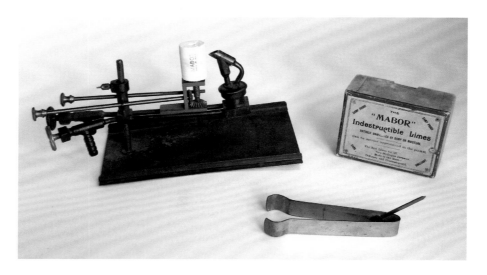

Limelight burner with limes and lime tongs

Almost immediately, commercial firms, particularly in London, began to produce new types of lanterns to take advantage of this increased light source. They also began to produce sets of lantern slides telling stories that could be used to entertain audiences. One of the first to mass produce slides was the firm of Carpenter and Westley in London. They made what they termed "Copper Plate Sliders", using techniques developed in the pottery industry to imprint the outline of images onto glass and with young female workers hand painting in the colours. Their first commercially produced set was a series of over 200 images on Natural History, showing the wide variety of animals, birds and fish found around the world. Carpenter and Westley are recognised today as slide and lantern makers of the finest quality. Their second commercially produced set of copper plate sliders was a set on astronomy, showing the major features of the solar system and constellations.

Fine Quality Brass and Mahogany Magic Lantern Circa. 1880

Throughout the 19th century the form of the lantern developed from a basic black metal body into a wide variety of styles. Hand made models of highly polished brass and mahogany became very popular in the UK. The continental manufacturers tended to work mainly with metal, although finishing the lantern in a blue metallic coating, known as Russian Iron, gave them a very attractive appearance. Lantern manufacturing also developed in the USA although it was the middle of the 19th century before large scale commercial production began. The use of a lantern with two or even three lenses and light sources became popular by the middle of the 19th century, allowing images to be superimposed and phased in/out of each other, creating spectacular effects.

Russian Iron Magic Lantern – Late 19th Century

The limelight burner had inherent dangers from burning a mixture of oxygen and hydrogen and many newspaper reports of accidents and explosions were recorded. Various alternatives were developed including substituting the hydrogen gas with ether or acetylene. However, both these methods had attendant dangers. In the 1870s carbon arc burners began to be introduced and the limelight burner phased out. Eventually, as the electric light improved it replaced the carbon arc. Throughout the history of the magic lantern, paraffin and oil burners were in use, particularly for home lanterns.

Lantern Slides

As the design of lanterns developed, so did the form of lantern slides. From it's origins until the 1880s all slides followed the basic design of glass with hand painted images. By 1850 most images were printed in outline and the colouring applied by hand. Mahogany frames were used to give strength.

From the beginning of commercial production, slides were produced in sets and normally came with a narrative or "reading". Many companies hired out lanterns, slides and all the necessary associated equipment. It would be possible to send a telegram to a supplier, ordering whatever slides and equipment were required from their catalogue and have them delivered by the railway company to the hall were the lecture was to take place. After the lecture the railway company would collect them and return everything to the supplier, with an invoice arriving a couple of days later. There are many stories of the disasters that could occur when the lecturer failed to prepare properly and relied on the printed reading to provide all the necessary knowledge. However, the availability of this relative low cost material allowed many people to provide magic lantern lectures without significant capital outlay.

It appears that for some time the difficulty and expense of producing photographic lantern slides meant that they were only produced in limited numbers. However, by the 1870s photographic slides were being produced in commercial quantities. By the 1880s photographic slides had largely replaced the hand painted images and the quality of photographic images allowed the slide size to shrink to 3.25 inches square.